THE STRUGGLE IS REAL,
BUT YOU CAN SUCCEED!

Dr. Shani Collins Woods

Also By Dr. Shani Collins Woods

INSPIRATIONAL

The SHE Devotional: 31 Daily Inspirations for a Woman's Spirit, Health and Emotions

Where the Battle is Won: 31 Daily Devotionals for Men of Faith

EDUCATIONAL

Applying to a Student Loan Forgiveness Program: A Guidebook

RELATIONSHIP

Healthy Love 365: A Fabulous Guide to Choosing Self-Love and Achieving Happiness in Your Relationship

DR. SHANI COLLINS WOODS

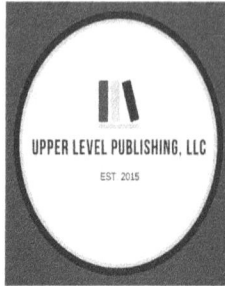

Editing by: EMG, LLC

Formatting: SC2, LLC

ISBN-10:0996923357

Paperback: 978-0-9969233-5-4

E-Book: 978-0-9969233-7-8

Printed in the United States of America

Note to the Reader

Although the author and publisher have made every effort to ensure that the information in this book was correct at press time, the author and publisher do not assume and hereby disclaim any liability to any party for any loss, damage, or disruption caused by errors or omissions, whether such errors or omissions result from negligence, accident, or any other cause. Some names and identifying details have been changed to protect the privacy of individuals.

Dedication

This book is dedicated to my mentors:
past, present, and future.
Thank you for sowing your wisdom into my life.

Acknowledgements

- To Jesus Christ, my Heavenly Father. For using me as a vessel, I thank you.

- To my parents, Mr. and Mrs. Charles and Cassie Collins, thank you for everything. I would be nothing without you.

- To my sister and brother, Kanika and Reginald, I love you both. Thank you for always being so supportive and open.

- To my nieces, Sidney and Baby S, and nephew, Reginald. Thank you for inspiring your aunt daily. No words can describe the happiness you bring into my world.

- The list of individuals who have prayed for and with me, cheered me on, put money in my hand, patted me on the back, given me a hug, a kiss, or a positive word is exhaustive. Thank you for encouraging me, showing me tough love, writing letters of support, making phone calls, advocating for me, and believing in me. Thank you for sowing into my life. Thank you for teaching me how to fly.

- To PC Designs LLC, thank you for the amazing book cover design. I can always count you on to bring my vision to life.

- To Emer, thank you for your meticulous editing. You are the best. SC, the formatting is great.

- To my many Facebook, Instagram and Twitter friends. I appreciate the constant support and online engagement.

- To the many individuals who purchased *The Struggle is Real, but You Can Succeed!,* thank you very much.

- Finally, to Timothy, my sweetheart, my husband, my best friend--this, I know:

If I ain't got nothing, I got you. If I ain't got something I don't give a damn, 'cause I got it with you. I don't know much about algebra, but I know one plus one equals two. And it's me and you. That's all we'll have when the world is through.

$-1+1,$ Beyoncé Knowles Carter

For free success tips, coaching, inspiration, and motivation, follow Dr. Shani Collins Woods:

Facebook Page	www.Facebook.com/AskDrShani
Instagram	@ASKDRSHANI
Twitter	@ASKDRSHANI
YouTube	@ASKDRSHANI
Podcast	http://askdrshani.libsyn.com/
Blog	WWW.ASKDRSHANI.COM
Personal Website	WWW.SHANICOLLINS.COM
E-mail and Speaking Inquiries	Info@shanicollins.com
Mailing Address	Upper Level Publishing, LLC Post Office Box 2184 Ridgeland, MS 39158

Contents

Introduction

For years, I have been teaching, speaking, and writing. Each year, and without fail, some young woman or man of color asks me: "Dr. Collins Woods, how did you do *this* or how did you do *that*?" I openly share my stories with people, especially young people, because I want them to have every opportunity to succeed. As much as we would like to think all people have equal-opportunities and equal-access to their *slice of the pie*, it simply is not true. Many young people of all racial and ethnic backgrounds fight educational, financial, gender, social, political, institutional, and systematic barriers on their path to success. With no mentors, many young people make avoidable mistakes.

In high school, I remember calling a prominent and powerful African-American female attorney from my hometown for assistance. I admired her. I saw myself in her. I said to her, "I want to become a lawyer. Can you please mentor me and share wisdom?" Annoyed with my question, she said, "Go ask someone else." I was crushed. She had the resources. She was black. She was visible in the community, yet, behind closed doors, she was unwilling to mentor me.

Some years later, I landed a job working at Hallmark

Cleaners. Each day, I saw Michael Moore, the former Attorney General of the State of Mississippi. He was always friendly, courteous, and nice to those of us who worked at the cleaners. One day, I mustered up the courage to ask him for help. Before he left the cleaners, I blurted out, "Hello Mr. Attorney General. My name is Shani Collins and I am a senior English major at Tougaloo College. I want to be a lawyer one day. May I please have an internship in your office?"

Without hesitation, he asked me for a slip of the cash register receipt paper. He wrote down one number and said, "Call this man on Monday." Within a few weeks, I was working for the Attorney General's office. You would think the chief lawyer for the state of Mississippi would be too busy for a college senior. He was not. He did not ask, "Who is this black girl asking me for a job?" No, he opened the door of opportunity to me. To this day, I remain grateful for that opportunity because it opened the door for me to work for the United States Securities and Exchange Commission when I relocated to Atlanta, Georgia following college.

Although I did not become a lawyer, I have accomplished many other personal and professional goals because I choose to keep praying, keep believing God has good things in store for me, and keep trying to succeed even when doors of opportunity are slammed shut in my face. That story about facing rejection from a hometown attorney and receiving a *yes* from the state's *most powerful* attorney is one example of many stories you will read in *The Struggle is Real, but You Can Succeed!* The stories I share are factual, and include simple truths that will help you stay focused on your personal and professional goals.

More than that, the 22 "Success Principles" I share in *The Struggle is Real, but You Can Succeed!* are a guide to help you know that the "Four G's"–faith in *God*, personal and professional *goals, guidance* from mentors, and personal *grit*–will help you rise above any challenge and succeed. Each chapter in *The Struggle is Real, but You Can Succeed!* has 2-4 "Discussion Questions" to help you apply critical thinking to your own journey toward success.

Here are a few things you will learn in this book:

- Why you need God to achieve true success.

- Why having a positive circle of influence is a major key to success.

- How learning from your mistakes increases your access to future personal and professional opportunities.

- Why ignoring your haters is integral to your success.

There is no straight path to success. No, the journey to achieving your goals will not be easy. However, by applying the "22 Success Principles" to your journey, you will attract peace, joy, happiness, fulfillment, and positive relationships into your life. In turn, the personal and professional success you want to achieve will be yours. And some years from now, you will look back on your journey and proudly say, "Yes, the struggle was real, but with God, goals, guidance, and grit, I succeeded!"

SECTION I:
Faith (God)

Honor God

"Commit to the Lord whatever you do,
and he will establish your plans."

–Proverbs 16: 3

S uccess is not something you can wish for. As a woman of faith, I know I can do nothing without God. Your success will not occur overnight. It requires hard work, focus, and discipline. Most of all, Godly success requires complete, total, and absolute surrender to God. I make it my purpose to ask God how I can use any project, assignment, platform, or activity to bring honor to His Kingdom. By doing that, God has opened amazing opportunities for me. If you will trust in God, and keep Him first in all things, you will be blessed.

This does not mean you sit back, pray, and do not work toward your goals. No, God has given you hands, eyes, ears, and feet. Use them all to research, study, learn, and hone your craft. When the time is right, and *if* your plans align with God's will for your life, your dreams will come to pass.

My mother instilled the importance of having

a relationship with Christ in me from a young age. I remember the exact day I gave my life to Christ. I was nine years old, attending Friendship MB Church. When Pastor Bozeman extended the invitation to Christ, I flew out of the choir stand. My older sister, Kanika, followed me. We were baptized and have been members of the church since.

My faith is everything to me. It has helped sustain me during times of trouble. I know I would not have achieved any of my goals if God was not involved in my life.

P1: DISCUSSION QUESTIONS

1. What role does your faith play in your life?

   _____

   _____

   _____

   _____

   _____

   _____

2. Do you seek spiritual guidance when making decisions about your life?

   _____

   _____

   _____

   _____

   _____

   _____

SUCCESS PRINCIPLE #2
Always Believe In Yourself

"Don't wait for permission to do
something creative."

–Ava DuVernay

Self-doubt kills many dreams. If your goal is to be a successful dancer, educator, writer, documentary maker, chef, or parent, your path starts with a sincere belief in God, but also in yourself. If no one around you believes in you, if others say, "You can't do it, you'll never amount to anything," you must have the courage to believe in yourself, always.

When you believe in yourself, you choose to believe what God says about you. In Jeremiah, He says, "Before I knew thee, I formed thee in the womb." This means God fashioned you with a purpose to carry out in your life.

Sometimes, trying new endeavors can fill us with doubt. We ask ourselves questions like, "Can I really do this?" "Do I have what it takes." Or, we compare ourselves to others and say, "Am I as good as Kate or Ted?" "I know I'll never be able to do it like she does or he does." When you have low expectations of yourself, you will manifest and project low or subpar outcomes.

For example, if you have studied hard to become a nurse or a realtor, and yet, you still think you cannot perform that job with excellence when the time comes, you will blunder your client visits, or you will never sell a single home. Wake up with an attitude that says, "God has equipped me with everything I need to succeed in life, or at this endeavor. I possess the knowledge, the skills, the determination to excel," and you will excel.

So be confident and do not doubt yourself. When you doubt yourself, you are really doubting that God equipped you with all you need to be successful.

P2: DISCUSSION QUESTIONS

1. Why is it important for you to not doubt yourself or your ability to succeed?

    _____

    _____

    _____

2. Engaging in the "comparison game" can cause you to doubt yourself. How can you avoid engaging in the comparison game, and focus on your own path?

    _____

    _____

    _____

3. Social media only gives us a snapshot of the lives of others. How can you combat feelings of inadequacy when you learn about the success of others?

    _____

    _____

    _____

Trouble Does Not Last Forever

"It's only temporary frustration."
–Dr. Cassie Osborne, Jr., Author's
Uncle

You may experience setbacks and disappointments on your path to success. Remember, trouble does not last always. So, keep an open mind about your troubles. Good and bad things happen to all of God's children. In the Word, it reads, it rains on the just and the unjust. How you handle your troubles says more about you, your faith in God, and your belief in your ability to *take a licking and keep on ticking.* Some people let setbacks stop them. You must be determined to always let your setbacks propel you forward.

Yes, I can tell you about setbacks in life. I have experienced my fair share of setbacks. The hardest one I have faced came three months before I earned my PhD. I had worked so hard to reach the point of defending my dissertation. In my mind, I was ready to graduate. After all, for seven years, I had been working toward my PhD, had passed several defenses, and committed many hours toward researching and writing my dissertation.

I saw June 2014 as my time to shine, and was anticipating an August 2014 graduation.

During summer 2014, I was completing a health disparities research training fellowship at Brown University, in Providence, Rhode Island. I was so excited about the opportunity to study at an Ivy League institution, and learn about clinical and translational research from some of the world's best research scholars.

A few days before my scheduled defense, I flew from Providence to my sister's home in Jacksonville, Alabama. The day before my defense, I drove to Tuscaloosa, Alabama and checked into a hotel.

The meeting started off okay. Over the years, I had learned to arrive early, and always have water and light refreshments for guests. I did just that. Slowly, my committee members arrived to the meeting. Then, a distractor walked into my meeting. He was a white male who was an administrator in the School of Social Work at the time. In front of everyone, he said, "Oh, I see you have goodies here to bribe your committee." This comment was highly offensive, but I ignored it, and was determined to stay focused.

I began my presentation and it went well. Then, I was asked a few questions about my research. I handled those questions well. Then, a question about my methodology caused my committee to pause. Then, my defense took a turn. I sat in silent awe as two of my committee members began arguing with each other across the table. All I could do was pray.

My chairperson asked me to step out of the room. When I returned, I was notified my defense did not pass.

Typically, this would have been the end of my career as a PhD student. My seven years of studying would have been down the drain. Ultimately, my committee members told me to meet again in three months for a second defense.

I went to my chairperson's office and sat there in disbelief and shock. My chairperson told me, "I would support you if you wanted to leave the program and not continue." I thought: "What? Is she really encouraging me to exit the program? What about all the years I have invested? What about my student loans?" I immediately told her quitting was not an option for me.

I was mortified, but I knew God was in control. I flew back to Providence to complete my training program and I met with Brown University professors for guidance and instruction. I presented my work in front of them, sat in their offices, had them assist me with any loopholes. One caring professor said to me, "Shani, when you return to Alabama, be sure to sever ties with one particular member of your committee. What you experienced should never have happened."

I could have let that major setback stop me, but I did not. I could have looked at the setback as an interruption in my graduation plans. It was, but there was always the next graduation. I decided I would hold my head high, that I would learn all I could while I was at Brown, that I would not look at the defense as the end. Instead, I would look at the re-scheduled defense as a "90 day" wait versus an indefinite pause.

When the second meeting came around, it was not even a meeting, it was more like a conversation.

There was no arguing between committee members. I was better prepared to defend my material. After the second defense, I still had work to do. I had revisions to complete. Yes, I was tired and somewhat traumatized by the experience. But, I finished what I had started. Was it easy? No. Did I experience letdowns, upsets, disappointments, and rejection? Absolutely.

Did the setbacks prevent me from landing a job? No, I was hired by Alcorn State University as an Assistant Professor, was accepted into a second research training program in Mississippi, and met many new mentors.

Remember, trouble does not last always. Do not get stuck in a pity-party. When life hands you lemons, remain humble. Remain focused. Feel your feelings (e.g. sadness, hurt, frustration, pain, anger, disappointment), and decide to push through anyway.

Later, I learned that several other individuals had a similar experience with their dissertation defenses. They also struggled to earn their degrees. But, in the end, they kept pushing forward. In the end, God rewarded their faithfulness. Today, we are all doctors.

1. What major setback(s) or disappointment(s) have you experienced? How did the setback or disappointment make you feel?

    _____

    _____

    _____

2. How can you remain resilient despite setbacks?

    _____

    _____

    _____

3. It is often said: "Behind every cloud is a silver lining." Although your setback or disappointment may feel like the *end of the world*, how can you find the silver lining in the situation?

    _____

    _____

    _____

SUCCESS PRINCIPLE #4

Forgive Others

It's one of the greatest gifts you can give to yourself, to forgive.

Forgive everyone." –Dr. Maya Angelou

To be successful, you must learn to forgive others. Throughout my life, I have met many people who mistreated me. I had to learn that holding on to anger about their actions toward me was unhealthy for me. For example, when I was in college, I had several encounters with female college peers and sorority sisters that were not positive. Those encounters were all about a man.

At the time, the gentleman I was dating, was dating other women. He was being dishonest with all of us. It was never my position to go confront a woman over a man. But, others confronted, menaced, harassed, and talked about me. During that time, I was hurt and felt alone. I felt that my boyfriend was a jerk and the women who were antagonizing me were jerks, too. Luckily, God freed me from that relationship and from that negative environment. In the end, I learned so much about people and dating choices.

Today, I have a loving husband. I forgave my ex-boyfriend and those women for their actions toward me. Most importantly, I forgave myself. In hindsight, we were all young, naïve, and clueless about life.

To succeed, learn to forgive. If you are holding on to pain from the past, ask God to show you how to let it go. Unforgiveness manifests itself in bitterness, anger, hostility toward others, cynicism, and a bleak outlook on life. It only blocks your progress, *your success*.

Someone who was your sworn enemy in high school or college may be your study partner or your business partner down the road. Forgive people for childish mistakes, learn from the past, and work on cultivating new experiences and positive relationships with people.

Unforgiveness is likened to drinking poison and expecting your enemy to die. When you forgive others, you allow God to use your life's testimony for His glory.

P4: DISCUSSION QUESTIONS

1. Why is forgiveness important to you?

   _____

   _____

   _____

2. Are there any people or situations you need to forgive?

   _____

   _____

   _____

3. How does unforgiveness hinder your spiritual, personal, physical, emotional, and professional growth?

   _____

   _____

   _____

4. When you forgive others, you do so knowing that others may not apologize for hurting you. Can you accept this truth and still be at peace?

_____

_____

_____

Have A Servant's Heart

"When I dare to be powerful—to use
my strength in the service of my vision,
then it becomes less and less important
if I am afraid."

–Audre Lorde

God purposed you to serve His kingdom and His people. Too often, we reach a level of success and forget about those left behind or those who have not reached our level of success. As you strive for success, remember to keep a servant's heart. Make a conscious effort to help those around you, those within your hometown/community, or even those with whom you work.

In my capacity as an educator, I am always called upon to offer guidance, advice or wisdom about topics. I try to encourage my students by first listening to them with an open heart. When they ask me questions, I respond to them with compassion. I seriously try to walk a mile in their shoes.

Sometimes, people do not really want money or advice, they just want to know that someone believes in them. I have found that being a support to others is a form of serving. But, if it is within your power to write someone a positive letter of reference, volunteer at the local community event, speak or share a word of inspiration or wisdom with the community, do so.

The world encourages us to be self-centered—"I" focused, and "self" focused. You will discover that you are blessed when you serve others. As you progress and grow, be humble enough to pause and focus on the needs, welfare, and concerns of others. Success shows people your character. Your character reveals who you are when no one is watching.

P5: DISCUSSION QUESTIONS

1. Who in your immediate environment (e.g. home, church, community, professional) can you serve or assist?

   _____

   _____

   _____

2. What are some ways you can serve others?

   _____

   _____

   _____

SECTION II:
Goals

Set Goals

> "If you're bored with life – you don't
> get up every morning with a burning
> desire to do things – you don't have
> enough goals."
>
> –Lou Holtz

You are reading this book because you want to succeed in life. That is great. As an educator, I observed that many people fail in life because they do not prepare to succeed. Therefore, goal-setting should be on your list of *Things to Do.* Goals give you a sense of purpose and direction. As a college professor, I meet many students who have no goals for being in college. They are enrolled in college to collect financial aid, to party, to find love, and sadly, to collect a refund check. This unique group has talent, but they are often unfocused in classes. They do not buy books. They drive nice cars, have the latest phones, but are spending 7-10 years in college simply because they have identified no other purpose. They have not set any realistic goals.

I vividly remember the summer before I enrolled in Tougaloo College. I was resistant to attending Tougaloo because so many of my relatives had attended the institution. Frankly, I wanted to attend a university that allowed me freedom to P-A-R-T-Y! Yes, I was 17 when I went to college. As a sheltered young lady, who did not get to hang out much, I wanted to live it up, party, and have fun.

I had not yet made a definite decision about college. One afternoon, my parents called me into our living room and I learned a valuable lesson about goals. My parents sat me down on the couch and said, "Listen, you are going to Tougaloo. We are not sending you anywhere else. You will declare a major when you enter. You will not be like those kids who never declare a major and jump from college to college. You will graduate in four years. Period. And, if you want to go somewhere else, we will not come to get you. Do what you want to do in graduate school."

Well, that matter was settled. That was one of my first lessons on goal setting. My parents did not leave my future to chance. Although I was a Highest Honors graduate and Miss Greenwood High, by my senior year, the college parties were on my mind. Knowing this, my parents set the goals for me: declare a major upon entering, graduate from one college, graduate in four years, and go to graduate school. I did just that.

Regardless of your age, you must set goals for your life. You cannot leave your life to chance. Set goals and work toward them. When you look back, you will realize that you are further along in life because you are working toward a specific goal. The fruit of your goal setting will inspire you to set and conquer more goals. So, what are your goals?

P6: DISCUSSION QUESTIONS

1. What are your "Top Five" goals?

   _____

   _____

   _____

2. What areas of your life are you most interested in improving and/or reinventing?

   _____

   _____

   _____

3. What is the biggest impediment to you reaching your goal(s)?

   _____

   _____

   _____

4. What efforts are you making to accomplish your goal(s)?

_____

_____

_____

SUCCESS PRINCIPLE #7
Do Not Despise Small Beginnings

"Start small, think big. Don't worry about too many things at once. Take a handful of simple things to begin with, and then progress to more complex ones.
Think about not just tomorrow, but the future. Put a ding in the universe."

–Steve Jobs

Success is not about having a fancy position every job you work at. Success is how you maximize the opportunities you have. For years, I worked as a secretary. For years, I was ashamed of being a secretary. Why? I always saw myself at the head of a company, doing more or leading my own team. I had a bigger vision for myself.

In some instances, I felt that some supervisors had a narrow definition of leadership and were not proponents of teambuilding. As I continued my career, I realized that having the opportunity to work under individuals in key leadership positions was an apprenticeship.

Instead of saying or thinking, "I hate being a secretary.

This position is beneath me," I used the position to learn all I could. I began to study, observe, and learn how to manage an office and manage employees. As the saying goes, "Most secretaries really run the office." It is true. I learned quickly that before people could talk to my boss, they had to talk to me. I also learned that I was in a unique position to meet key people of influence. It was in my positions as a secretary that I learned the importance of building relationships with people.

Additionally, I learned to research things. If I did not know an answer, Google was always handy. My small beginnings as a secretary taught me so much about humility, leadership and teamwork. You see, achieving success is not an overnight process.

Most successful people have worked their way up from the bottom to the top. By itself, the title Chief Executive Officer (C.E.O.) means nothing. To be a real C.E.O., you must be able to apply your knowledge and skills to projects, to team building, and to a larger vision. After all, there are many people who are C.E.Os in name, but who lack the skills and insight needed to run a successful organization. In other words, C.E.O. is mindset. Whatever you put your mind to, you can do.

Today, I can proudly say that being a secretary was the best thing for me. It really prepared me to be organized in my doctoral program (e.g. remember meetings, being prepared for meetings). The research skills I acquired as a secretary also benefitted me as a professor (e.g. I am very resourceful). Small beginnings teach us a lot about our character. If you can serve in a position that you do not like, and do it to the best of your ability, God will elevate you in due time. Do not allow your season of small beginnings to be filled with complaining and negativity. You may not be where you want to be today, but your starting point does not have to determine your ending point.

Remember, others are watching how you behave in your dry season. Use the small beginnings to teach you what you need to know about the goals you have set for yourself. It is important to learn, grow, and acquire skills before you leap into certain positions. Small beginnings are necessary for growth.

Notables like Oprah Winfrey were not made in one day. Before she was Oprah Winfrey, the legend, she was a news anchor in Tennessee. She used that experience to help her establish her own brand, and later the Oprah Winfery Network (OWN).

1. It is often said, "You have to crawl before you walk." What does that statement mean to you?

   _____

   _____

   _____

2. Social media gives the illusion it is possible to become an *overnight success* What do you think of becoming an *overnight success*? It is something you strive to become? Why or why not?

   _____

   _____

   _____

3. Bishop T. D. Jakes of the Potter's House once said, "I started my ministry in a storefront church with no plumbing and no roof." Why is it easy for us to only focus on people's glory and overlook their *small beginnings?*

   _____

   _____

   _____

4. How can you learn to be more humble while God increases your territory?

_____

_____

_____

Learn To Be An Independent Thinker

"The most courageous act is still to
think for yourself. Aloud."

–Coco Chanel

A major impediment to people's success is not
being an independent thinker. As a person of
faith, being an independent thinker is about
more than not following the crowd. It's about following
God's prompting and direction for your life, and
knowing when an opportunity is for you.

Here is an example of why you should think
independently. Prior to my enrollment in the University
of Alabama, I reached out to various academic professors
about my interest in earning a doctoral degree. One
professor told me, "You know, you may want to think
about going somewhere else and doing something
different." I was thinking, "But why? This is what I
want to do and I am trying to get a perspective." I also
had an uncle advise me against attending the university
because of institutional racism.

I told myself this: "God is everywhere. Yes, racism,
especially institutional racism, is alive and well, and no

institution is without blemish. But, if God allowed my foremothers and forefathers to earn PhDs in the 1900s and 1920s when times were far less racially progressive, and when they did not have the Internet, cell phones, or access to research infrastructure, and they still succeeded despite of those barriers, so can I."

In that moment, I realized that my life decisions could never be rooted in other people's fears.

I would encourage you to learn to think independently about your life decisions. This does not mean you dismiss people's advice and do not consider their experiences as valid. You must know that their experience may not be *your experience*. You cannot allow other people's fears to hold you back from making decisions about your life. Had I not attended the University of Alabama, I would have missed out on a valuable, rigorous, amazing, and nearly *free* educational experience. Roll Tide!

1. Being an independent thinker is crucial to your success. Do you let the opinions of others dictate your actions?

_____

_____

_____

2. Most successful leaders have wise counselors nearby. Do your counselors consult God's wisdom before they advise you?

_____

_____

_____

3. Do you seek God first in your decision-making?

_____

_____

_____

SECTION III:
Guidance

SUCCESS PRINCIPLE #9
Acknowledge Your Village

"The youth can walk faster, but the elder knows the road."

–African Proverb

Honor your mother and father. Your parents made you. They love you and want to see you succeed. Often, when we are riding the wave of success, we forget about the people who changed our diapers, fed us, clothed us, prayed for us, helped us graduate from high school and college, helped us buy our first home, and helped us start a business.

On your path to success, do not forget about your parents, or those who have helped you along the way. When your parents or any seasoned adult asks you to assist them, help them if it is within your power. Too often, young adults take, take, and take some more. And, they never give back to their parents.

Giving back does not have to be in the form of money. You can give back with your time. Drive your parents to the doctor. If you live with them, keep the house clean, assist with chores, cook dinner, babysit, assist in the church or community, make good grades, get a job to help pay bills, buy your own clothes, go to college and graduate in a timely manner, start a business, and make something of yourself.

There were many times when I could not give back to my parents. During my graduate school years, I faced financial insecurity. Often, I could not give back the money my parents had given me. But, I served in church and did whatever I could to be helpful at home and in the community.

Parents like to see their children *trying* to make a difference in their lives. They want you to do something positive and stay off the streets.

Your parents are making sacrifices because they want you to do better in life. Think of ways to honor them while you can. Most of all, when you overcome "the struggle," don't exclude them from your awards speeches, your graduation ceremony, or recognition programs.

When you have the platform, after you acknowledge God, publicly thank and acknowledge your parents. If they are like my parents, they may not want the spotlight. But, give them their flowers while they are here. Let the world know you did not reach success by yourself. Let the world know who your parents are and who your village is. One day, you parents will go home to be with the Lord. Value your time with them, appreciate and acknowledge them, spoil them when you can, and treat each day with your mother and father as if it were your last. After all, they deserve it.

P9: DISCUSSION QUESTIONS

1. Who are the members of your support system?

   _____

   _____

   _____

2. Do you think it is important to express appreciation to the members of your support system? Why or why not?

   _____

   _____

   _____

3. How do you show appreciation to your support system?

   _____

   _____

   _____

4. If you have overlooked any member of your support system, what can you do to avoid repeating this behavior in the future?

_____

_____

_____

SUCCESS PRINCIPLE #10
Be Mindful Of Your Circle Of Influence

"The idea behind the circle of influence is simple. The more time we spend around people who work hard, set goals, and push forward, the more likely we are to pick up their positive traits. At the same time, if we surround ourselves with underachievers, we may end up picking up negative traits."

–Gerard Adams, *Entrepreneur*

Several years ago, I asked my social work students from Alcorn State University to make a list of their top five friends. I did this because, as a professor, I recognized that my students were not maximizing their full potential. I concluded that their associations were distracting them from focusing on their most important goal: graduation.

I asked them to think about the lives their college friends led, what their plans were, and where their friends were headed. Then, I told them: "You become like the people with whom you associate." I added: "If your friends are going nowhere, you will be headed down that same path if you do not make a change."

The room fell silent. Visibly emotional, one of my students stopped me while I spoke to the class. She said, "Dr. Collins Woods, you are so right. I'm so sorry because I know I am a better student, but I have been having so many friendship and relationship issues that I can't focus on my school work. I am an A student." As a professor, I already knew that their learning barriers were less about their ability to comprehend and master the concepts and more about their circle of influence.

Your circle of influence matters. Your *circle* should consist of people who think highly of themselves, exhibit self-respect to you and others, and honor themselves with positive choices. When I was in college, my friends and I looked out for one another. Today, many of my friends are successful lawyers, doctors, dentists, pharmacists, educators, counselors, health professionals, researchers, and entrepreneurs.

We had goals for our lives. Did we have personal struggles and regretful experiences in college and graduate school? Sure, we all did, but life is about learning from your mistakes and moving forward. By God's grace, we all managed to stay focused enough to finish undergraduate, graduate, and professional school.

You should also have goals for your life. Most importantly, you should associate yourself with people who have a quest for living and who are *about the business*. This does not mean you behave arrogantly toward others who may not have life figured out just yet. Yes, you can encourage them, but it is not your job to fix everyone's life.

Remember, you are a chosen child of the Most High King. God has provided His bible to give you clear direction for your life. In the book of Proverbs, He advises us to be mindful of the company we keep. As a woman on her personal grind, I am very mindful of the energy around me. I have a low tolerance for negative vibes, negative energy, confusion, strife, and discord. I like to keep it positive, hang around fun, upbeat, centered women and men who are unashamed to walk in their purpose.

Do a gut check. Better yet, make a list of your "Top Five" friends. Do you want to go where they are headed? If so, great. If not, consider making changes with yourself and with your associations. You cannot *change* the people around you, but you can change *which* people are around you.

1. Who are the top five individuals you associate with?

   _____

   _____

   _____

2. What are their plans for the next two, three, five years?

   _____

   _____

   _____

3. Where are their plans for achieving spiritual, personal, financial, and professional success?

   _____

   _____

   _____

4. Do any members of your circle of influence tempt you to stray off the path God has chosen for you? If so, what will you do about this individual(s)?

_____

_____

_____

Choose A Godly Mate

Then the Lord God said, "It is not good for the man to be alone. I will make a helper who is just right for him."

-Genesis 2:18

Do not date a non-supportive person. Why? On your path to success, you will need a supportive partner. You will need a shoulder to cry on, someone to give you sound advice, someone to give you an objective perspective, and someone to help you unwind after a bad day. Most of all, you will need a prayer partner. When I experienced various in-school challenges, I longed for a person to pray with me, to talk to about the *struggle*, and to be a support system for me.

You will need prayer more than money, affection, movies, dinners, and "Netflix and chill," when the going gets rough. You do not need someone posting, "Pray for my girlfriend or boyfriend on Facebook." No, you need someone who can pray for you and who is willing to stand in the gap for you, especially when you are trying to accomplish a large goal.

You cannot achieve success alone. Your parents' support is different than the support of a partner who loves you and wants to see you succeed. When you are going through the fire, facing meetings alone, standing alone as the only woman or man in the room, standing as the only African American, the only Christian, the youngest, the pressure will take a toll on you. You will need respite in the Lord, and in a partner who can help you see Christ during your trial.

If your partner only offers an occasional pat on the back, or does not support you in the way you feel you need to be supported, say thanks, but no thanks. You need and deserve more than that. You need a Godly mate who will stand in the trenches with you and go before the throne with you during your time of struggle and triumph.

If your partner chooses to not stand with you during your struggle, you do not need him or her around when you experience victories in life.

P11: DISCUSSION QUESTIONS

1. In what ways can having a Godly mate help you on your path to success?

   _____

   _____

   _____

2. In what ways can having an ungodly mate hinder your path to success?

   _____

   _____

   _____

SUCCESS PRINCIPLE #12
Mentorship Matters

"A mentor is someone who allows you
to see the hope inside yourself."

–Oprah Winfrey

I am a proud member of Delta Sigma Theta Sorority, Inc. Clubs and organizations are a wonderful way to meet new people, socialize, and fulfill a larger commitment to that organization's mission. When you are involved with or are undertaking a serious task like finishing a college, undergraduate, graduate and/or terminal degree, those connections will come in handy. I have learned the importance of having professional mentors.

For example, I secured my first collegiate level teaching because I met a Tougaloo College alumna. Keep connections and stay in touch with people from your high school, college, and graduate school. Relationship building is important. If you do not have a mentor, seek to cultivate a relationship with one.

Identify a person who is already where you want to be. Reach out to that person, ask questions, and ask the individual if he or she is willing to share wisdom with you. Do not be the person who only calls on your resources when you need them. No, keep them updated on important aspects of your life. Send them emails, letters, an occasional text, and simply call them to say hello. Everyone needs a good mentor. A mentor or a person with more experience, leadership, and connections can help you navigate through the professional world. I love my mentors and know that I would not be where I am today without their guidance.

P12: DISCUSSION QUESTIONS

1. Who are the members of your mentorship team?

   _____

   _____

   _____

2. Some people are afraid to ask for help or to seek out a mentor. How can you overcome being shy, timid, afraid, or even prideful and ask to be mentored?

   _____

   _____

   _____

3. Once you have a mentoring team, what are the most effective ways for you to cultivate and maintain a positive relationship with your mentoring team?

   _____

   _____

   _____

SUCCESS PRINCIPLE #13

Do Not Compare Yourself To Others

"Someone else's success doesn't equate to your failure."

—Anonymous

The premise of this book is that you will experience some form of struggle on your journey to success. Struggle is to be expected. Your struggle may not look like the next person's struggle. It can appear as though others are succeeding, winning, and achieving more in their lives. This can cause you to feel jealous, discontent, and disheartened. Remember, you must stay focused on your journey. You must be able to celebrate with others and know that your day will soon come.

Life is not a competition. It is a journey. Some people will marry, have kids, buy a home, and/or launch a business in a matter of a few years. Others will face divorce, miscarriage, foreclosure, business failure, and extreme poverty before they reach their life goals, but they persevere until they do.

Do not focus your energy on what others around you are doing. Instead, focus your attention on what God is doing in your life, on fulfilling the purpose He has for your life, and controlling what you can control. Setbacks will happen. That is why *the struggle is real*. Any measure of success you achieve will come from God's favor and the sweat of your own brow.

Do not lose heart. Do not get discouraged on your journey. Most of all, do not sit back, look at the lives of others, and wish for their success. You may be complaining about your lack of this or that, and look at someone's life in envy. You may see their glory, but you may not know their story. Do you really know what is going on behind the scenes in their lives? Do you really know if their success was earned in an honest way?

Focus on your own path. Be confident that you are living out your passion. Know that some people's success also includes years of struggle and strain. Everyone may not share their "struggle phase," but they have had one.

P13: DISCUSSION QUESTION

Michael Phelps said, "Winners focus on winning. Losers focus on winners." How can you apply that quote to your life and your own vision of success when others around you are aspiring to do the same exact thing as you?

_____

_____

_____

_____

_____

_____

_____

_____

SUCCESS PRINCIPLE #14
Be A Team Player

Teamwork: simply stated is less me and more we."

--Anonymous

The maxim goes, "Team work makes the dream work." This is very true. Being a team player will help you achieve much success in life. There have been times when I felt I was a great member of an awesome team and we flourished.

For example, earning my PhD required that I spent days and evenings working with my cohort members and professors. Often, we were assigned group projects. For the most part, I never experienced any group conflict. Everyone knew how serious our work obligations were. There were times when my peers and I had to share notes, exchange ideas, and deal with challenging information. The goal was for everyone to succeed. Luckily, we all graduated and are now doing what God has called us to do in our respective careers. Presently, I am a member of an excellent research training program that has excellent team dynamics.

You will experience challenges. There were times

when I was a member of teams and organizations that did not embrace the "team model." Usually, those teams had reached a plateau where no new information and ideas could be given, exchanged, or received. Operating in that space is not productive. If you achieve all the dreams and desires of your heart, you will not do it alone. You will need a team of people to help you sustain your vision. Learn how to adopt a team mentality. By learning to work well with others, you will go further in life.

1. George Shinn, owner of the Charlotte Hornets said, "There is no such thing as a self-made man. You will reach your goals only with the help of others." Consider Mr. Shinn's statement within the context of P14. How important is teamwork to you?

_____

_____

_____

2. Do you work well in team environments?

_____

_____

_____

3. Reid Hoffman, LinkedIn co-founder, said, "No matter how brilliant your mind or strategy, if you're playing a solo game, you'll always lose out to a team." What does this quote mean to you?

_____

_____

_____

SUCCESS PRINCIPLE #15
Diversity Matters

"No one is born hating another person because of the color of his skin or his background or his religion. People must learn to hate, and if they can learn to hate, they can be taught to love, for love comes more naturally to the human heart than its opposite."

–Nelson Mandela

I have met several people who will not visit certain doctors because they are not from their same racial/ethnic background, or who will not associate with people who are not members of their same sorority or fraternity. Group affiliations are important, but they are not the end all or be all any situation. Do not stop living your life just because the people involved in an activity with others do not look like you, sound like you, or share the same racial/ethnic or group affiliation as you. Most of all, do not turn down God given opportunities because you fear being the only woman, the only member of a racial/ethnic group, or *the only* in any group. Someone must break down barriers, right? Why not you?

I am a two-time HBCU grad. While studying Tougaloo College and Clark Atlanta University, I was around individuals who shared my racial background and many other cultural similarities. When I attended the University of Alabama, I was in a much more diverse environment. Often, I was the only African American female in class. I had good and bad days at all three institutions.

Learning to work with diverse groups will be instrumental to your success in life. We do not live in a monolithic society. It is good to experience diversity in food, cultures, to study diverse topics, and to keep an open mind when making and establishing relationships. The person you reject because they do not look like you or share your same "affiliation," may be the very person God is using to bless your life, and/or take your career to the next level.

P15: DISCUSSION QUESTION

How can having an "open-mind" about diverse people, places, foods, cultures experiences, views, religions, help you grow as a person?

_____

_____

_____

_____

_____

_____

_____

_____

SECTION IV:
Resilience (Grit)

Learn To Speak Up
For Yourself

"People violate you when you don't
have clear boundaries because you
don't tell them how to behave in
your life."

–Iyanla Vanzant

It is important for you to learn the power of your voice. It is important for you to learn to speak up for yourself. To be successful, you will sit among people from all walks of life. Some will share your same ideas and philosophical views, others will not. Some will be more vocal, more competitive, more aggressive in meeting their bottom line. Others will not. Your responsibility is to use your voice.

For a while, I took the position that I did not want to "step on people's toes." On occasion, I have smiled through others' insults, dealt with their mischaracterizations of me, and *turned the other cheek* to their disrespectful attitudes. It is never okay to silence your voice to make others feel better about themselves.

I was enrolled in graduate school with a young

woman I knew from college. In fact, when she was applying to UA's graduate program, she emailed me and asked me to help her craft her personal statement for her PhD program. I happily obliged. The first week of starting our individual PhD programs, we went out to eat and I bought her a devotional book.

She had never vocalized a problem with me. However, when we hung out in social settings with our other peers, she would often direct snide or sidebar remarks toward me or attempt to discredit me in the eyes of others.

I would usually leave our dinners irritated with her. I began to ask myself, "What is her behavior about?" I was very silent for a while. Then, I mentioned my inter-actions with her to my mother who said to me, "When you get tired of her, you'll speak up for yourself." She was right. I did speak up for myself. I did express to her how her behavior was inappropriate and not "cool," and how no one in our group appreciated her behavior.

I learned that having boundaries is healthy for any relationship. That was just one example of a "frenemy" situation, but I also learned to speak up more in meetings, in the classroom, and when in a group setting. In academic settings, some of your peers will quickly assert their dominance or "strut their stuff" because they want an A, to land the internship, or the job. It is true that many professors are drawn to students who appear to be engaged in their classes. Or if you are in a business or professional setting, supervisors are drawn to those individuals who share ideas and who are outspoken about showing support for their team's vision.

Whether you are defending your character, or making it clear that you are in the room by participating and engaging with others in an academic or professional setting, know that your voice is powerful. It is relevant. It is important. And, you deserve to be heard.

1. Have you ever experienced an incident where you did not speak up for yourself?

    _____

    _____

    _____

2. How did not speaking up for yourself make you feel?

    _____

    _____

    _____

3. How can you learn to speak up for yourself and/ or assert yourself, yet not burn bridges with the individuals in your personal or professional circle?

    _____

    _____

    _____

4. How do you determine when it is time to move on from relationships that make you feel bad about yourself?

SUCCESS PRINCIPLE #17
Know Your Worth

"No one can make you feel inferior
without your own consent."

–Eleanor Roosevelt

From a very early age, I began telling myself that my self-worth and self-esteem would never be based on the opinions of others. I still hold on to this truth today.

God created you to do wonderful things for His kingdom. Some people will love you, accept you, be drawn to you, and support you. Other people will hate your guts for no apparent reason.

You must be so confident and secure in yourself first as a Child of God. You must know that you are covered and that no weapon formed against you will ever prosper. Having positive self-esteem will help you make wiser decisions about your life's goals. When you make decisions from a place of having high self-esteem, you will make decisions that truly honor you and those around you.

If your decisions are emanating from a place where you think you are worthless, or where you think bad thought about yourself, you will dishonor yourself in negative ways.

Yes, life will knock you down and throw things your way that will nearly crush your self-esteem. You will encounter negative people who will sap your joy, who will tell you that you are not good enough, that you are too ambitious, that you are not what "the company wants," and even that you are over underqualified for certain positions.

Just know that negative news or a blow to your self-esteem is the perfect opportunity for you to grow into a stronger, more determined, more resilient version of yourself. During a job interview, a black male academic told me I had "been in school too long." This comment unnerved me because I worked hard to earn every degree I have. I did not know it was a crime to be smart and ambitious. I did not land that job. Ironically, six months later, an African American female administrator who works for the same organization said: "We would *love* to have you as a member of our team." Regardless of what others say, never base your self-esteem on their opinion. You are valuable and you have what it takes to succeed!

P17: DISCUSSION QUESTIONS

1. What does self-worth mean to you?

   _____

   _____

   _____

2. In what ways is your self-worth tied to your interpretation of personal and/or professional success?

   _____

   _____

   _____

Learn From Your Mistakes

"Your greatest teacher is your last mistake."

–Unknown

One of the most important lessons I learned occurred during my senior year of college. Having been hired for an internship, I was excited at the prospect of attending law school. I knew the internship would complement my resume. The office work load was minimal. As such, there was a lot of down time. At the time, I was assigned to work in the office of a woman on maternity leave.

Because I had also worked in my uncle's law office, I had grown accustomed to using his office supplies, answering his telephone calls, picking up an occasional book to read, accessing his files, and grabbing an occasional legal pad to write on. When I worked for this organization, I made a terrible mistake of making calls on their line. I was not calling friends, family, or goofing off on their line. Instead, I was calling out-of-state law schools to request materials, etc.

One day, I was told to come to a meeting about

something. In that meeting, I was notified that the woman whose office I was using reported me for using her phone. The gentleman she reported me to told me this: "An ounce of prevention is worth a pound of cure." He was right. This was not my uncle's office. Although I was trying to advance my education, using the office phone to make calls was not the wisest decision. I think the calls totaled to $30.00. I paid the fee and continued the internship. Lesson learned.

Could the woman have told me directly? Did she miss an opportunity to mentor me? I believe so. She could have told me about the matter in person, but her intent was to remove me from the position. Because she was on maternity leave, I think she felt I would take her job.

I never reported her two-hour lunch breaks or her office shenanigans. The lesson is not about what other people do, the lesson I learned was to be mindful of what I did when I was entrusted with others' property. I did not have a bad attitude about being corrected. I took it as a lesson learned and I grew from it. I carry that lesson with me today.

You will encounter people who operate by their own professional and moral standards in the workplace. They may come and go as they please. They may use the Internet, office supplies, and materials for their own purposes. They may allow their co-workers, spouses, relatives, friends, and family members, or students to lounge around the office. They may never hold themselves accountable for any of their unprofessional ways. As a child of God, you must hold yourself to a higher standard.

If you work in an environment where the rules are laxed, be very cautious to avoid slip-ups. I have learned that people may not monitor what they do in relaxed environments, but they will monitor *what you do*. In environments where the standards are high, everyone is held accountable for their actions.

To this day, I do not move many personal things into new office spaces. And, I limit my use of office property (e.g. telephone, computer, furniture, etc.) to work related matters only. I do not become too comfortable or relaxed in any professional environment.

You will make mistakes on your journey. Some of your mistakes will be small, others will be large. But, the best way to overcome a mistake is with a humble attitude, with an apology, and with and attitude and behavior that demonstrate you have learned the lesson. That incident occurred over 15 years ago. I graduated and moved on from that position. The woman who reported me still works there.

1. We have all made mistakes. What is the greatest lesson you have learned from your personal and/or professional mistakes?

    _____

    _____

    _____

2. How can learning from your mistakes make you a sharper, wiser person both personally and professionally?

    _____

    _____

    _____

SUCCESS PRINCIPLE #19
Let Your Haters
Motivate You

"The cynics may be the loudest voices, but I promise you, they will accomplish the least."

–Barack Obama

"When they go low, we go high."

–Michelle Obama

Recently, I watched the August 26th boxing match between Floyd Mayweather (49-0, 26 KOs) and UFC champ, Conner McGregor (21-3, 180KOs).

I did not get a chance to see the fighters' weigh-in. Excited about the fight, I headed over to YouTube to watch the weigh-in on the UFC's channel. I watched both competitors, armed with large security details, strut their stuff and officially weigh in.

They both made weight and moved about the stage. McGregor was interviewed by a reporter. He mainly talked a lot of trash about Mayweather. Trash talk is to be expected; it is the nature of the marketing, ticket sales, hyping up the audience, and being a celebrity. Trash talk equates to tweets and re-tweets, social media posts, and viral content. When the reporter spoke to Mayweather, he was calm, poised and unnerved during his interview. When he was asked about the fans and the overwhelming support for McGregor, he said, "Fans don't win fights. Fights win fights."

His statement resonated with me. He was absolutely right. In life, your haters or the people who do not support you have no power to determine your personal success at any endeavor. Yes, your haters or distractors may make noise, attempt to distract you from your purpose, and talk trash about you. Ultimately, it will be your personal dedication, commitment to your goals, professionalism, and expertise that propel you to the next level in life.

When you are faced with your distractors, brush their comments off and stay focused. Then, remember Floyd Mayweather's words: "Fans don't win fights. Fights win fights." In the end, Floyd Mayweather won the fight against Conner McGregor, retained his title as the undisputed lightweight boxing champion of the world, and set a new all-time record: 50-0.

P19: DISCUSSION QUESTIONS

1. On Oprah's Lifeclass, she recalled the wisdom Dr. Maya Angelou gave her about haters. "In the beginning, it used to bother me so much when people would talk about me," Oprah said. "She used to say to me, 'Baby, those people can't hold a candle to the light that God already has shining on your face.'" What does this inspirational quote from Mya Angelou mean to you?

   _____

   _____

   _____

2. What is your strategy for dealing with haters?

   _____

   _____

   _____

3. Oprah Winfrey said she never responds to haters because it gives her power away. Haters can say mean, wicked, and vile things about us and mistreat us. Why is it important to keep your power and apply your energy to constructive things versus engaging your haters with a response?

_____

_____

_____

SUCCESS PRINCIPLE #20
Don't Procrastinate

"You pray for rain, you gotta deal with the mud, too. That's a part of it. I'd be more frightened by not using whatever abilities I'd been given. I'd be more frightened by procrastination and laziness."

–Denzel Washington

I always say to myself: "Shani, procrastination is you standing in your own way." It really is. To be successful, you must learn to do things in a systematic way. This does not mean your life has to be planned out to the letter, but it does mean you have a system in place that allows you to get things done in an effective and efficient way. Ultimately, this means you limit procrastination.

Honestly, we put off things because we do not think they are a priority. For example, if I perceive that watching a reality television show is more important than cleaning my home, I will put it off. In short, we procrastinate because we see the alternative option as less challenging than the project or task we should be undertaking.

The wiser thing would be to create a schedule that allows me to clean and watch television, too. This way, the imperative thing—keeping a clean home—is handled while I do something I enjoy: watch television.

When it comes to business success, procrastination gives others a bad impression of you. People will want to know that you are responsive, responsible, and capable of getting things done on time.

You may say, "Well, I work best under pressure." I do not believe that. I think pressure is healthy, but it also causes people to overlook details, rush, and not operate in excellence.

For example, I hired a wedding coordinator. I did not know she was a procrastinator. She did not have things done months before our wedding. It caused problems for me, the decorator, the catering crew, the church, and the venue. She was frustrated, overwhelmed, and on our wedding day, made several inexcusable blunders. These were problems I did not create.

Luckily, God allowed our day to run smoothly. My point is: when you procrastinate, not only do you stand in your own way, you also place more stress on yourself. If you are working with other people, you create drama and chaos that does not have to exist.

As you move forward, learn to create a schedule and try to stick to it. If you are someone who chooses to do things your own way, on your own time schedule, just know that your lackadaisical methods will catch up with you in the end and will cause you to lose personal/

professional relationships and/or business. No one wants to work with a person who does not have respect for their time.

1. Do you procrastinate? If so, why?

   _____

   _____

   _____

2. How has procrastination delayed one or more of your personal and/or professional goals?

   _____

   _____

   _____

3. What are some of the ways you can prioritize your tasks to avoid procrastination?

   _____

   _____

   _____

Speak Truth To Power

"The most common way people give
up their power is by thinking they don't
have any."

–Alice Walker

As a graduate student at Clark Atlanta University (CAU), my classmates and I learned the true meaning of "fighting my way" out of a bad situation. I love CAU. My experience at CAU made me mentally tough and it 100% prepared me for the PhD program at the University of Alabama. I say this because I had to advocate for myself as a student.

When I graduated Tougaloo College, I did not have the best plan in place. I was not accepted into law school and did not have a job, so I applied to graduate school. Clark Atlanta University accepted me. So, by August 2003, I was a full-time graduate student, living in a new city, and studying in an entirely new discipline: Africana Women's Studies. I loved the major because I learned so much about myself, women's rights, feminism, and patriarchy. Some of the concepts were new to me. Others were familiar, but I did not know the academic term. I remember learning about feminism and thinking, "Oh, you mean my mother and all of my aunts? This is who they are! This is who I am!"

I advanced through the program. What should have been a two-year program ended up being a four-year stay at CAU and a lot of student loan debt. People get master's degrees in 18 months. I was growing frustrated. I did not know that my classmates were, too. The problem centered on our Department Chair. The Chairperson was older, did not have the faculty support, resources, and infrastructure to manage theses and dissertations in an efficient way. This meant that many people were being "held up" in our department. To add, there was a level of resistance to change. Old habits die hard sometimes. In an academic environment, the students are often at the mercy of the professor.

In my case, it was time to graduate. I had passed my Comprehensive Exams, had written my thesis, had my thesis defense, and because of Committee conflict, was being held up in the process. Initially, I did not want to "rock the boat." I did not want the professor to think my concerns were personal. In an HBCU environment, we sometimes violate boundaries because the environment is so family-oriented. Sometimes, professors do not do right by students and students do not do right by their professors. In this case, I quickly realized the importance of committee dynamics. If you have the wrong committee members on your team, you will be the innocent bystander who gets wounded.

From that experience, I learned how to leverage the power of positive mentors. I learned how to speak for myself and how to let my professors speak for me. Most importantly, I really learned how to stand still and let God soften people's hearts. I learned how to document, document, document, write letters, and be strategic about advocating for myself and my rights as a student in an academic program. In the end, the Dean had to become involved. My struggle was minimal compared to my peers. Others had to resort to legal action to graduate. Essentially, they did what they had to do. In my opinion, if a student has all of the requirements, a professor can't arbitrarily tell them they cannot graduate. I began to apply to PhD programs. Guess what, I was accepted!

The lesson I learned from Clark was that you cannot fear your professors or others in power. You must be assertive about what you want, speak up for yourself, and know that being on the side of right may mean you lose relationships. You have to be okay with speaking up for yourself. Had I not taken some action, I would likely have dropped out of the program, started over somewhere else, or worse, just left and been stuck with the student loan debt.

When you pursue a new endeavor, do your research first. Would I choose Clark Atlanta again? Yes, indeed. Would I have done more research on certain aspects of that program and applied for more scholarships? Yes.

I left with my sanity, but I also entered into my PhD program with a letter in hand from that Chairperson stating that I would graduate in July 2007, just enough time for me to start my program in August 2007.

1. Why is it hard to speak truth to powerful people?

   _____

   _____

   _____

2. When we speak truth to power, we can transform environments. Have you considered using your voice to change the environment around you?

   _____

   _____

   _____

SUCCESS PRINCIPLE #22
You Must Never Quit

"Freedom! Freedom! I can't move.
Freedom, cut me loose!

Freedom! Freedom! Where are you?
Cause I need freedom too!

I break chains all by myself.
Won't let my freedom rot in hell.

Hey! I'ma keep running.
Cause a winner don't quit on themselves."

–Beyoncé Knowles Carter

It was 2009. My father had just been diagnosed with prostate cancer. I was second year PhD student then and I was worried, busy traveling, somewhat disorganized, and tired. The second year of your PhD program is the hardest. It is when you really delve into your coursework. It is when you start to feel the reality of what you have committed to.

I remember going to class one day and not being spot on. In a PhD program, the class sizes are small, so your absence is noted if you miss a session. If you come in late, your tardiness is noted. If you are not prepared, your lack of unpreparedness is noted and obvious.

When 30 students are in a class, you can get by with not answering. If the professor is moving around the class room, you can quickly Google an answer, or read up on materials before it is your turn to respond. But when you are one of 2 or 3 students in the class, and when you are in that class for three hours, the spotlight is on you. The professor has prepared and she or he expects you to be prepared with no excuses. On this occasion, I did not have it together in class.

Knowing that I was unprepared, I wanted to meet with the professor and apologize. I did just that. I asked to meet with him. I explained that my dad was sick and that I had a lot of different things going on. I apologized.

He told me, "You should drop out of the program." I was thinking: "Wait, what? I just told you my father has cancer and I am adjusting to the new news and your response is to quit the PhD program?" I didn't go any further with the conversation. I somehow told him that I was disinterested in quitting and would see him in class. That was my last conference with that professor.

That meeting was on a Friday. Discouraged, I packed my bags and headed home to Greenwood. It was the only refuge I had. My parents and sister were there. Mad, I said, "You know what, this is not for me. I should quit. When we return to campus after the break, I am going to have my "drop out" letter ready for him."

I mentally planned my exit strategy as I drove home. As the sun set, I passed a small church on my right. I had grown fond of reading their church signs as I traveled into and out of Tuscaloosa. The sign read:

"Many people want the harvest, but few people want to sow." Instantly, I got it.

There I was complaining about my PhD program being too hard. Yes, it was normal for me to be upset about my dad's cancer diagnosis, but his cancer was also diagnosed in Stage 1; it was treatable.

No, the professor should not have told me to drop out. That was discouraging and disheartening to hear during a time when I needed to be reassured that I was welcome at the university and the department.

As I have stated over again, to succeed, you have to learn to compartmentalize people's actions and their words. You have to know what to hold on to and what to let go of. The professor was telling me how he felt. That was his truth. I had to realize that dropping out or quitting early could not be my truth.

I did not quit the program. Instead, when I returned to class, I came to class prepared. I did not have any excuses. I kept my personal problems separate. At the end of the day, the professor did not care about my father anyway.

You will face challenges. Your parents will get sick. Your loved ones who have been a part of your life will die. Tragedy will happen. People will not respond the way you think they should. On the other hand, you will have some people to love you, to cry with you, and to hold your hand.

Whether you have the support or not, you must determine in your mind that you will not quit when tragedy strikes your life. It is advisable to take time to grieve, mourn, and distance yourself from anything that is just too heavy for your plate.

But do not let someone's harsh words, their ill-treatment of you, or their callous advice to quit what you have started stop you for accomplishing your goal. If God says stop then stop; otherwise, learn to let bad advice go in one ear and out the other. In the words of Winston Churchill: "Never, never, never give up!"

1. Life can get tough. Why must you not give up on your goals?

   _____

   _____

   _____

2. What mantra or Scripture inspires you to not quit when life gets tough?

   _____

   _____

   _____

About the Author

Dr. **Shani Collins Woods** is a bestselling author, motivational speaker, and the Founder/ CEO of Shani K. Collins Consulting, LLC. She has authored several books including *The SHE Devotional: 31 Daily Inspirations for a Woman's Spirit, Health and Emotions, Where the Battle is Won: 31 Daily Devotionals for Men of Faith, and Healthy Love 365: A Fabulous Guide to Choosing Self-Love and Achieving Happiness in Your Relationship.* Shani and her husband, Timothy, make their home in Mississippi. Visit her at: www.shanicollins.com.